Minds Through Time:

A Journey Through the History of Psychology

Freudian Trips

Copyright Page

Disclaimer

The views and opinions expressed in this book are those of the author(s) and do not necessarily reflect the official policy or position of any other agency, organization, employer, or company. The contents of this book are for informational and educational purposes only and are not intended to serve as professional advice, diagnosis, or treatment.

The information provided in this book is believed to be accurate and reliable as of the date of publication. However, it may include some errors or inaccuracies, and no warranty or guarantee is provided regarding the accuracy, timeliness, or applicability of the content.

Readers are encouraged to consult with professional philosophers, educators, or other qualified professionals where appropriate for personalized advice. The author(s) and publisher shall not be liable for any loss, damage, or harm caused or alleged to be caused, directly or indirectly, by the information or ideas contained, suggested, or referenced in this book.

By reading this book, the reader acknowledges and agrees that they are solely responsible for how they interpret and apply the information contained herein.

This book may also include references to other works, studies, and sources. These references are provided for further reading and exploration and do not imply endorsement or validation of the specific theories, viewpoints, or interpretations presented in those works.

Introduction

Hello, dear reader, and welcome to an exciting journey through the fascinating world of psychology. But you might be wondering, what is psychology? Well, psychology is the study of the mind and behavior in its most basic form. It's a field that seeks to understand how we think, feel, and act, both as individuals and in groups. It's about understanding what makes us tick, why we do the things we do, and how we can change for the better.

Psychology is everywhere. It's in the way we communicate with our friends, how we perform at work, and even how we fall in love. It's in the advertisements we see on TV, the social media posts we scroll through, and the decisions we make every day. In essence, psychology is the science of us, and that's what makes it so fascinating!

Why Study the History of Psychology?

Now, you might be wondering, why should we study the history of psychology? Isn't it enough to understand the current theories and practices? Well, to fully appreciate the field of psychology, it's essential to know where it came from.

Studying the history of psychology allows us to see how our understanding of the human mind and behavior has evolved over time. It helps us appreciate the contributions of the many brilliant minds who have shaped the field and understand the context in which they worked. It also allows us to learn from past mistakes and avoid repeating them in the future.

Moreover, the history of psychology is not just a dry list of dates and names. It's a captivating story full of intriguing characters, groundbreaking ideas, and dramatic shifts in thinking. It's a tale of human curiosity, ingenuity, and the relentless pursuit of knowledge. And by studying it, we become part of that story.

The Scope of This Book

In this book, we will embark on a journey through the history of psychology, from its ancient beginnings to the cutting-edge research of today. We will explore the key theories, concepts, and figures that have shaped the field, and look at how they have influenced our understanding of the human mind and behavior.

We will delve into various branches of psychology, including psychoanalysis, behaviorism, humanistic psychology, and cognitive psychology, among others. We will also look at how psychology has been applied in various fields, from education and healthcare to business and marketing.

But don't worry, you don't need to be a psychologist or a scholar to enjoy this book. We've made sure to present the information in a clear, engaging, and accessible way, free of jargon and complex terminology. Whether you're a student, a professional, or just a curious reader, we hope this book will spark your interest in psychology and inspire you to learn more about this fascinating field.

So, are you ready to embark on this journey? Let's dive in and explore the fascinating world of psychology together!

Chapter 1: Ancient Beginnings

Early Psychological Thought: Prehistoric and Ancient Civilizations

Welcome to the dawn of psychological thought! Our journey begins in the distant past, long before psychology was formally recognized as a discipline. In prehistoric times, our ancestors were already grappling with questions about human behavior and the nature of the mind.

They may not have had the scientific tools we have today, but they were keen observers of human behavior. They recognized patterns, made connections, and developed theories to explain why people behaved the way they did. These early insights laid the groundwork for the development of psychology as we know it today.

Moving forward to ancient civilizations, we find that many societies had their own interpretations of psychological phenomena. The Egyptians, for example, believed that the heart was the center of emotion and thought, while the ancient Chinese attributed mental health to the balance of yin and yang forces in the body.

Philosophy and Psychology: The Greek Influence

As we move into the era of ancient Greece, we find the birthplace of Western philosophy, which has had a profound influence on psychology. Great thinkers like Socrates, Plato, and Aristotle began to ask questions about the nature of the mind, knowledge, and human behavior.

For instance, Plato proposed a tripartite model of the soul, dividing it into the rational, spirited, and appetitive parts. Aristotle, on the other hand, emphasized the importance of observation and experience, laying the groundwork for empirical methods in psychology.

These Greek philosophers set the stage for many of the questions that psychologists would continue to grapple with for centuries to come. Their influence is still felt in the field today, reminding us of the deep roots of psychological thought.

Eastern Philosophies: Psychological Aspects of Hinduism, Buddhism, and Confucianism

While Western philosophy was taking shape, equally profound psychological insights were emerging in the East. In the philosophies of Hinduism, Buddhism, and Confucianism, we find rich explorations of the mind and human behavior.

Hindu philosophy, for instance, introduced the concept of the 'self' and explored the idea of consciousness. Buddhism, with its emphasis on mindfulness and the nature of suffering, offers insights that have been integrated into modern therapeutic practices. Confucianism, with its focus on social relationships and moral development, also provides a unique perspective on human behavior.

These Eastern philosophies remind us that psychological thought is a truly global phenomenon, with diverse cultural perspectives contributing to our understanding of the human mind and behavior.

As we close this chapter on ancient beginnings, we see that the seeds of psychology were planted long ago, in different soils around the world. These early insights, born out of human curiosity and the desire to understand ourselves, have grown into the rich field of psychology we know today. As we move forward in our journey, we'll see how these ancient beginnings have shaped the course of psychological thought, leading us to new discoveries and deeper understandings.

Chapter 2: Emergence of Modern Psychology

The Birth of Modern Psychology: Wilhelm Wundt and the Establishment of the First Psychology Laboratory

As we move forward in time, we arrive at a pivotal moment in the history of psychology: the birth of modern psychology. This period is marked by the work of Wilhelm Wundt, a German scientist often referred to as the "father of experimental psychology."

In 1879, Wundt established the first psychology laboratory at the University of Leipzig in Germany. This was a significant milestone as it marked the separation of psychology from philosophy and its establishment as a scientific discipline in its own right. Wundt's laboratory was a place where experiments were conducted, data was collected, and theories were tested - a model that modern psychology still follows today.

Wundt's work focused on understanding the structure of the mind through introspection, a method where individuals reported their own conscious mental experiences. This leads us to our next topic: Structuralism.

Structuralism: Understanding the Mind's Components

Structuralism, as the name suggests, was an approach that sought to understand the structure of the human mind. It was pioneered by Edward B. Titchener, a student of Wundt, who brought Wundt's ideas to the United States.

Structuralists held that the mind could be dissected into its fundamental parts in a similar way to how a scientist dissects objects. They used introspection to identify these elements, aiming to create a "periodic table" of the mind's components.

While structuralism provided valuable insights, it also faced criticism. Its reliance on introspection was seen as subjective and unreliable, and it was criticized for focusing too much on the parts of the mind without considering how they work together. This led to the emergence of a new school of thought: Functionalism.

Functionalism: A Response to Structuralism and the Influence of Darwinian Thought

Functionalism emerged as a response to the limitations of structuralism. Instead of focusing on the structure of the mind, functionalists were interested in understanding the purpose or function of mental processes.

Inspired by Charles Darwin's theory of evolution, functionalists believed that our mental processes must have evolved for a reason - to help us survive and adapt to our environment. They sought to understand what these functions might be and how they could explain our behavior.

Prominent functionalists like William James and John Dewey argued that psychology should study the mind as it operates in the real world, not just in the controlled conditions of a laboratory. This emphasis on practicality and application has had a lasting impact on psychology, influencing areas like educational, industrial, and clinical psychology.

As we close this chapter on the emergence of modern psychology, we see how the field has evolved from its philosophical roots to a scientific discipline. The debates between structuralists and functionalists set the stage for the diverse approaches and perspectives that characterize psychology today. As we continue our journey, we'll see how these early schools of thought have paved the way for the many branches of psychology that exist today.

Chapter 3: The Psychoanalytic Revolution

Sigmund Freud: The Father of Psychoanalysis

As we turn the page to a new chapter in the history of psychology, we encounter a figure who would forever change the way we think about the mind: Sigmund Freud. An Austrian neurologist by training, Freud is best known as the father of psychoanalysis, a revolutionary approach to understanding human behavior and treating mental disorders.

Freud's work was groundbreaking. He proposed that our behavior is driven not just by our conscious thoughts and feelings, but also by desires and fears that lie in the unconscious part of our mind, hidden from our awareness. This was a radical idea at the time, challenging the prevailing belief that we are fully aware of the forces that drive our behavior.

The Conscious and Unconscious Mind

Central to Freud's theory is the concept of the conscious and unconscious mind. The conscious mind, according to Freud, is like the tip of an iceberg. It represents our current thoughts, feelings, and perceptions - the mental processes that we're aware of.

Below the surface, however, lies the vast and powerful unconscious mind. This is the realm of desires, fears, and memories that have been repressed or forgotten. According to Freud, these unconscious forces can influence our behavior in ways we're not aware of, leading to symptoms like anxiety, depression, or unusual behavior.

Freud developed techniques like free association and dream analysis to explore the unconscious mind, aiming to bring these hidden forces into the light of consciousness. This process, he believed, could help people understand and resolve their psychological difficulties.

Critiques and Contributions of Psychoanalytic Theory

Freud's theories were controversial and sparked intense debate. Critics argued that his theories were difficult to test scientifically, relied too heavily on sexual and aggressive drives, and painted a rather pessimistic picture of human nature.

Despite these criticisms, Freud's impact on psychology is undeniable. He challenged the prevailing views of his time, broadened our understanding of the mind, and introduced new methods for treating mental disorders. His work has influenced a wide range of areas, from art and literature to philosophy and cultural studies.

Moreover, the concept of the unconscious mind has been integrated into many modern psychological theories, and psychoanalytic therapy has evolved into a range of psychotherapeutic approaches used today.

As we close this chapter on the psychoanalytic revolution, we see how Freud's bold ideas have sparked controversy, inspired further research, and enriched our understanding of the human mind. His legacy reminds us that psychology is a field that continues to evolve, driven by the relentless curiosity and daring ideas of its pioneers.

Chapter 4: Behaviorism Takes the Stage

From Introspection to Observable Behavior: The Rise of Behaviorism

As we continue our journey through the history of psychology, we encounter a significant shift in focus. From the introspective methods of structuralism and the deep dives into the unconscious mind by psychoanalysis, we now turn to a school of thought that emphasizes observable behavior: Behaviorism.

Behaviorism emerged in the early 20th century as a reaction to the introspective methods used by earlier psychologists. Psychology, according to behaviorists, should be a science of behavior rather than the mind, and ideas should be founded on observable and quantifiable conduct rather than introspection or unconscious forces.

John B. Watson: The Founder of Behaviorism

The founding figure of behaviorism is John B. Watson, an American psychologist who believed that psychology should study what people do, not what they experience or feel. Watson argued that behaviors are learned responses to environmental stimuli, and that by changing the environment, we can change behavior.

Watson's work laid the groundwork for behaviorism, but it was his successor, B.F. Skinner, who would become the most influential figure in this school of thought.

B.F. Skinner and the Influence of Operant Conditioning

B.F. Skinner, another American psychologist, expanded on Watson's ideas and developed a more comprehensive theory of learning based on reinforcement and punishment, known as operant conditioning.

Skinner proposed that behaviors followed by positive outcomes are likely to be repeated, while those followed by negative outcomes are not. This simple but powerful idea has been used to explain a wide range of behaviors, from learning to speak a language to quitting smoking.

Skinner's work has had a profound impact on psychology and beyond. His ideas have been applied in many areas, including education, therapy, and even animal training.

Despite criticisms that behaviorism overlooks the role of thoughts and feelings, its emphasis on observable behavior and experimental methods has helped make psychology a more rigorous and empirical science.

As we close this chapter on behaviorism, we see how this school of thought has shaped psychology's focus on observable behavior and the environment's role in shaping it. As we continue our journey, we'll see how these ideas have paved the way for later developments in the field.

Chapter 5: Humanistic Psychology and the Focus on the Self

The Emergence of Humanistic Psychology: A Third Force

As we delve deeper into the history of psychology, we encounter a school of thought that brought a fresh perspective to the field: Humanistic Psychology. Humanistic psychology, which first emerged in the middle of the 20th century, was frequently referred to as the "third force," setting it apart from the two then-dominant schools of thought, psychoanalysis and behaviorism.

Humanistic psychology shifted the focus from the unconscious mind and observable behavior to the individual's subjective experience. It emphasized the inherent goodness of people, the importance of personal growth, and the pursuit of self-fulfillment.

Carl Rogers and the Person-Centered Approach

One of the key figures in humanistic psychology was Carl Rogers, an American psychologist known for his person-centered approach.

According to Rogers, everyone has an inherent need to self-actualize, which is the process of realizing and expressing one's own skills and creativity.

Rogers emphasized the importance of empathy, unconditional positive regard, and genuineness in helping individuals grow and fulfill their potential. His person-centered approach has had a significant impact on psychotherapy, counseling, education, and other fields.

Abraham Maslow and the Hierarchy of Needs

Another influential figure in humanistic psychology was Abraham Maslow. He is best known for his theory of the hierarchy of needs, a model that describes the different levels of needs that humans strive to meet.

Maslow's hierarchy of needs places fundamental physiological requirements like food and water at its base. Following the satisfaction of basic wants, people try to satisfy higher-level needs like safety, love and belonging, esteem, and ultimately self-actualization.

Maslow's hierarchy of needs has been widely used in various fields, including education, business, and healthcare, to understand human motivation and personal development.

As we close this chapter on humanistic psychology, we see how this school of thought has enriched our understanding of human nature. It reminds us of the importance of personal growth, self-fulfillment, and the positive aspects of human experience. As we continue our journey, we'll see how these ideas have influenced later developments in psychology.

Chapter 6: Cognitive Revolution and the Return to Mind

The Cognitive Revolution: The Mind Re-enters Psychology

As we progress through the history of psychology, we arrive at a pivotal moment known as the cognitive revolution. This was a period in the mid-20th century when psychology shifted its focus back to the mind, after decades of emphasis on observable behavior.

The cognitive revolution was a response to the perceived limitations of behaviorism. Psychologists began to realize that to fully understand human behavior, they needed to explore the mental processes that underlie it. This led to a renewed interest in perception, memory, problem-solving, and other aspects of cognition.

Information Processing and Memory: Understanding How We Think

One of the key developments of the cognitive revolution was the information processing model of cognition. This model likens the mind to a computer, with inputs being processed and transformed into outputs.

A central focus of this model is memory. Psychologists sought to understand how information is encoded, stored, and retrieved in our minds. This led to the development of influential theories, such as the multi-store model of memory, which proposes separate stores for sensory, short-term, and long-term memory.

Cognitive Neuroscience: The Intersection of Psychology and Neurology

The cognitive revolution also paved the way for the emergence of cognitive neuroscience, a field that combines psychology and neurology to explore how brain activity underlies mental processes.

With the advent of technologies like functional magnetic resonance imaging (fMRI), researchers can now observe the brain in action, providing insights into how different regions of the brain contribute to cognition.

As we close this chapter on the cognitive revolution, we see how the return to the mind has enriched our understanding of human behavior. The cognitive approach has provided valuable insights into how we perceive, remember, think, and solve problems. As we continue our journey, we'll see how these insights have shaped modern psychology and continue to drive its future.

Chapter 7: Contemporary Psychology: From Theory to Practice

The Growth of Applied Psychology

As we move closer to the present day in our exploration of psychology's history, we see the field expanding beyond theory into practical applications. This shift is marked by the growth of applied psychology, a branch that uses psychological principles and research to solve real-world problems.

Clinical psychology, educational psychology, industrial-organizational psychology, and other fields are all included in the field of applied psychology. These fields aim to improve people's lives by addressing mental health issues, enhancing learning and teaching, improving workplace productivity, among other goals.

Positive Psychology: The Science of Happiness

Another significant development in contemporary psychology is the emergence of positive psychology. This field, championed by psychologist Martin Seligman, focuses on the positive aspects of human experience, such as happiness, optimism, and resilience.

Positive psychology seeks to understand what makes life worth living and how individuals can lead fulfilling, meaningful lives. It has led to new approaches in therapy, education, and self-help, emphasizing strengths and virtues over deficits and disorders.

Cross-cultural Psychology: Acknowledging Cultural Differences in Psychological Phenomena

In our increasingly globalized world, psychology has also recognized the importance of cultural context. Cross-cultural psychology investigates the impact of cultural influences on thought and behavior.

This field acknowledges that psychological phenomena are not universal but can vary across cultures. It seeks to understand these differences and their implications, contributing to a more inclusive and diverse understanding of human psychology.

As we close this chapter on contemporary psychology, we see how the field has evolved to address real-world issues, promote well-being, and acknowledge cultural diversity. These developments reflect psychology's ongoing commitment to enhancing our understanding of the human mind and behavior and applying this knowledge for the betterment of society.

Chapter 8: Psychology and the Future

Emerging Trends in Psychology

As we look towards the future of psychology, we see several emerging trends that promise to shape the field. One of these is the increasing focus on prevention and early intervention in mental health, moving away from a purely treatment-oriented approach.

Another trend is the growing recognition of the importance of mental health in overall well-being. This is reflected in initiatives to integrate mental health care into general health care settings and to address mental health issues at the community level.

Interdisciplinary Approach: Where Does Psychology Meet Other Sciences?

The future of psychology also lies in its intersection with other disciplines. The interdisciplinary approach recognizes that complex human phenomena cannot be fully understood from a single perspective.

For instance, the field of social neuroscience combines psychology, neuroscience, and sociology to explore how social processes affect the brain and vice versa. Similarly, behavioral economics integrates psychology and economics to understand how cognitive biases influence economic decisions.

The Role of Technology and Artificial Intelligence in Psychology
Technology is another factor shaping the future of psychology. Digital technologies are revolutionizing the way psychological services are delivered, with teletherapy and online mental health resources becoming increasingly common.

Artificial intelligence (AI) also holds exciting possibilities for psychology. AI can help analyze large datasets, identify patterns, and make predictions, potentially enhancing our understanding of human behavior and mental processes.

As we close this chapter and our journey through the history of psychology, we see a field that is continually evolving and adapting. The future of psychology holds exciting possibilities, with new trends, interdisciplinary collaborations, and technological advancements promising to further enrich our understanding of the human mind and behavior.

Conclusion: Reflections on the Journey

The Relevance of History in Modern Psychological Practice

As we conclude our journey through the history of psychology, let's reflect on the relevance of this history in modern psychological practice. Understanding the evolution of psychology provides context for current theories and practices. It helps us appreciate the diversity of approaches in psychology and the ongoing debates that shape the field.

Moreover, the history of psychology reminds us that our current understanding of the mind and behavior is built on the work of many thinkers across time and cultures. It encourages us to approach psychological knowledge with humility and curiosity, recognizing that our understanding will continue to evolve.

The Importance of Psychological Literacy for All

This journey through psychology's history also underscores the importance of psychological literacy for all. Psychological literacy refers to the ability to apply psychological principles to personal, social, and global issues.

In an increasingly complex world, psychological literacy can help us navigate our relationships, make informed decisions, and contribute to societal well-being. Whether we are psychologists or not, understanding psychology can enrich our lives and our communities.

Concluding Thoughts

As we close this book, we hope that you've gained not only knowledge about psychology's history but also an appreciation for the discipline of psychology itself. We've traveled from ancient philosophies to modern theories, from introspection to neuroimaging, from the individual mind to cultural contexts.

This journey is a testament to the richness and diversity of psychology, and to the human curiosity and quest for understanding that drive this field. As we look towards the future, we can expect that psychology will continue to evolve, offering new insights into the human mind and behavior.

Thank you for joining us on this journey through the minds and times of psychology. Here's to the continued exploration of the human psyche!

About Freudian Trips

Welcome to Freudian Trips, your dedicated platform for diving deep into the world of psychology. We are more than just a YouTube channel or a book publisher. We are a beacon of enlightenment, making complex psychological concepts accessible and engaging for all.

Our YouTube channel is a rich repository of psychology made simple. We take the profound and often complex ideas from the world of psychology and break them down into digestible, easy-to-understand content. From the foundational theories of Freud to the cognitive insights of Piaget, we cover a broad spectrum of psychological schools and thoughts, making psychology accessible to everyone, regardless of their background or prior knowledge.

As a book publisher, we take the same approach, transforming intricate psychological theories into comprehensible narratives. Our books are not just collections of words, but vessels of wisdom that make psychology approachable and relatable. We believe that psychology should not be confined to academic circles, but should be available to all who seek to understand the human mind and behavior.

At Freudian Trips, we believe in the power of curiosity and the pursuit of knowledge. We are here to stoke the fires of your curiosity, to guide you on your intellectual journey, and to help you navigate the fascinating world of psychology.

If you are someone who is not afraid to question, to explore, and to learn, then you are in the right place. Join us on this journey of exploration, as we make psychology easy to understand, one concept at a time.

Be sure to visit our Youtube channel at:
   www.freudiantrips.com/youtube

You can also visit us on the web at www.freudiantrips.com

Welcome to The Freudian Trip community. Stay curious. Stay enlightened.